Air Fryer Cool UK

Simple and Delicious Recipes with Coloured Pictures

By Evie Harrison

TABLE OF CONTENTS

INTRODUCTION

Air Fryers have started to become popular, due to the fact that you can avoid many of the unhealthy aspects of modern cooking. But what is an Air Fryer exactly, and how on earth does it work?

Air Fryers are basically an upgraded, enhanced countertop oven, but they became popular for one particular reason. In fact, many of the manufacturers, such as Philips, market this machine solely based on the claim that the Air Fryers accurately mimic deep-frying, which, although extremely unhealthy, is still very popular in this day and age (as it is, in my opinion, one of the most delicious ways to eat food).

Air Fryers work with the use of a fan and a heating mechanism. You place the food you want cooked in a basket or on the rack, turn on the machine, and the Air Fryer distributes oven-temperature hot air around your food. It provides consistent, pervasive heat evenly to all the food within. This heat circulation achieves the crispy taste and texture that is so tantalizing in deep fried foods, but without the unhealthy and dangerous oil! Both have been replaced by this miracle machine with hot air and a fan.

ADVANTAGES TO USING AN AIR FRYER

I may have already slipped in a few of the advantages to using an Air Fryer, but now let's expand a little more on everything an Air Fryer can do for you. After all, no investment should be made unless it's absolutely worthwhile.

And in truth, the Air Fryer is very worthwhile. I cannot begin to tell you how the advantages start piling up; this is not just another average appliance that everyone is getting because of a simple trend. People are getting Air Fryers because of their incredible, numerous, multifaceted benefits.

There are, however, a few notable advantages of using an Air Fryer, which I'll list below. If you don't know anything else about Air Fryers, I hope that these will convince you of their worth.

HEALTHIER COOKING

This is perhaps the top benefit that comes with air frying. In a society that really struggles with healthy cooking, we can use all the help we can get. Luckily, Air Fryers make it easy, all while maintaining many of the factors that make unhealthy food delicious!

Air Fryers use very little oil, which is one of the best ways to replace those unhealthy fried foods, like fried chicken, potatoes, and so many others. If you are like me (a lover of deep fried foods) then this is the answer to your dilemma of healthy eating while still enjoying the crispy taste of food!

Do keep in mind that you still need to spray fried foods, such as fish, with a touch of oil to make sure it does get evenly crispy. All in all, however, there is no denying the amount of oils is a whole lot less.

This singular change makes all the difference in the world. Healthy eating has never been easier, as you'll get the same crispy and flavoursome results, with minimal amounts of added oils. You'll even be able to "fry" foods you never were able to before—the possibilities are endless!

SAFER AND EASIER

Nothing scares me more than a hot pot of oil. It is an accident waiting to happen, and getting struck with burning oil splatters is no joke! But this, and its corresponding injuries, is often the price to pay for deep fried foods.

Air Fryers are also user-friendly, and this makes a huge difference. You don't have to feel like you are studying for a degree when working with an Air Fryer. Making dinner is far less complicated in an Air Fryer than many of the traditional methods of cooking. For some meals—unless you choose one of the more complex recipes I'll share later—you can even revert to placing a small piece of meat (even if it happens to be frozen!) into the basket and select the cooking settings.

The simplicity of the Air Fryer is its beauty. You will save countless time and unnecessary frustrations, and still make delicious food!

FASTER THAN COOKING IN THE OVEN

Once you buy an Air Fryer and set it to heat for the first time, you won't know what hit you! The average normal oven needs about 10 minutes to preheat. Due to the Air Fryer's smaller size and innovative design, it will be ready to go in no time!

It's even faster during the actual cooking. With the circulation that allows your food to be cooked crisp and even, it cuts a whole lot of cooking time out of the equation. This is amazing, especially in this day and age where technology, work, friends, family, and even pets are constantly demanding our attention.

Just imagine! You could set your food in the Air Fryer, and (with some recipes) it will be ready to eat in less than 20 minutes!

SAVES SPACE

If you are someone living in a small apartment, or a student accommodation, then an Air Fryer is perfect for you. Air Fryers are much smaller in comparison to a conventional oven and you can easily make use of this Air Fryer in 1 cubic foot of your kitchen.

You can even pack your Air Fryer away after use if need be, but the majority of people choose to keep it out on the counter. But it's nice to have the option to move your Air Fryer around if space becomes an issue.

LOW OPERATING COSTS

Considering how much cooking oil costs these days and the amount you need to use, you will soon be cutting costs in making deep fried foods. All an Air Fryer uses is a small amount of oil and some of the electricity to power up the Air Fryer, about the same amount that a countertop oven would.

Not only will you be cutting out the massive oil costs, which will save money, you will likely also save money by ordering out less, as you'll be able to replicate your favourite foods quickly and easily at home!

NO OIL SMELL

In reality, smelling like the food you just ate is not impressive, regardless of how delicious the food may be. This is what often happens, however, when people enjoy deep fried foods.

When deep frying foods, it also causes the whole house to smell, and as the oil splatters around, it can leave a massive mess. The oil can even harden on the walls, causing grime to build up into a nasty concentration of dirt and grease.

With less cooking oil, Air Fryers don't have any of those oil smells and keeps the space cleaner around you, as all the oils, smells, and actual cooking are contained within the machine.

PRESERVES NUTRIENTS

When you are cooking your food in an Air Fryer, it actually protects a lot of the food from losing all its moisture. This means that with the use of a little oil, as well as circulation with hot air, it can allow your food to keep most of its nutrients which is excellent for you!

If you want to cook healthy foods with the purpose of maintaining as many nutrients as possible, then an Air Fryer is perfect for you!

EASIER TO CLEAN

Cleaning is perhaps the bane of my existence, especially after cooking and having a long day. This can really take away a lot of the pleasure of making yourself a great meal. But an Air Fryer lightens the burden by being easy to clean!

Consistent cleaning after using it (much like any pot or pan) can allow for easier and simpler living. You just need some soapy water and a non-scratch sponge to clean both the exterior and the interior of your Air Fryer. Some Air Fryers are even dishwasher-safe!

GREAT FLAVOUR

The flavour of Air Fryer "fried" foods is nearly identical to traditional frying, and the texture is exact. You can cook a lot of those great frozen foods, such as onion rings or french fries, and still achieve that crunchy effect. This certainly can help you turn to healthier foods, especially if your goal is for healthy but quality meals.

The Air Fryer helps to cook your food to perfect crispness, instead of the soggy mess that happens when you try alternative methods of cooking foods that are meant to be deep fried (like chicken tenders). No one really enjoys mushy food. The Air Fryer keeps that desired element while remaining healthy.

All you will really need is just some cooking oil sprayed outside of your food to end up with a cooked interior and a crunchy exterior. So no worries! You still can eat your foods with a crunch and a healthier result!

VERSATILE

Unlike rice cookers meant just for rice, or bread makers meant just for bread, you will find that an Air Fryer leaves a lot of room to be both versatile and healthier. You can cook almost anything you would like in the Air Fryer (as long as it fits). From spaghetti squash, to desserts, even to fried chicken! You will probably never run out of air frying options!

VARIOUS TYPES OF AIR FRYERS AND HOW TO CHOOSE THE ONE FOR YOU

There isn't one standardized choice of Air Fryers, which means you are far more likely to find an Air Fryer that really suits your particular needs. Whether it be size or price, you have a wider variety of choices than what normally comes with conventional ovens.

So what are the key aspects that you need to take into consideration when getting yourself a nice Air Fryer? Let's begin:

- **Dimensions:** Obviously they come in different sizes, and despite saving space, some can still be bulky. When thinking about your countertop, you do want to consider its size and dimensions. You don't want to play a game of tilt with your Air Fryer, nor have it taken up all the extra space you have!

- **Safety Features:** You may want to check that it has an auto shutoff, as it is certainly a desirable feature. Air Fryers can get very hot during use, and an auto-shutoff can save you a lot of stress and fire emergencies. Furthermore, having a cool exterior can prevent potential red and burnt hands. So do yourself a favour and make sure they have all these elements at hand.

- **Reviews:** Naturally, this is the best thing to check out. Considering that the businesses rarely give out all the information, you will certainly find it out when people leave reviews. The customer hides nothing, and if they are unhappy, they make sure everyone else knows about it. However, if people are very happy, many of them will also note it in the reviews, and it is best to target the Air Fryers that tend to have the high reviews.

TWO COMMON DIFFERENCES

Beyond those functional differences, there are two mainstream designs of Air Fryers: basket Air Fryers and oven Air Fryers. Each has very unique and distinguished features in which to enjoy. Let us take a look at the differences between the two:

BASKET AIR FRYERS

Basket fryers are known to need less space than oven Air Fryers, which is very practical if you have limited space. Not only does it save space, but it also saves time, as the food is quickly heated up (without unnecessarily heating up the kitchen). Unlike an oven Air Fryer, and the larger traditional oven, it only takes about 1-2 minutes for the basket Air Fryer to heat up, and it is quite easy to place the foods inside of the basket.

The cons are, for one, that it does make a lot more noise than the oven Air Fryer. You also will not be able to watch the food as it cooks, which can increase the chances of burnt food if you are not careful. Also, a basket Air Fryer may not be the best if you need to cook a lot of food, as it is limited in capacity. This means that batch cooking may be required if you need a large amount of food.

This makes a basket Air Fryer ideal if you have a limited budget, don't need to cook a huge amount of food, and have limited free time. They are quick, small, and convenient, especially perfect for people who are students or single working professionals, and maybe even you!

OVEN AIR FRYERS

Oven Air Fryers, in contrast, have a larger capacity, which means you can cook a lot more food at the same time. They also have multiple functions for cooking and cut down on the noise than the basket Air Fryer. You will also be able to move the food closer or even further away from the heating element. There is a lot more flexibility involved in the use of an oven Air Fryer. Best of all, you can place parts of the oven Air Fryer into the dishwasher to be washed (thus cutting down the cleaning process, if you happen to have a dishwasher).

But, do be aware that it takes up more counter space, and takes a larger initial bite out of your wallet. It may also heat up the kitchen more, and if you are in fashion and aesthetic design, it might be disappointing to find out the colours and themes are more limited than basket Air Fryers.

These are the two main common types of Air Fryers; however, there are new types of Air Fryers that are coming to light for you to use and enjoy, most notably, the paddle-type Air Fryer. This version has a paddle that moves through the basket of your Air Fryer in order to help circulate hot air in between each piece of food.

This saves you the effort of pulling your food out at a specific time and shaking or stirring it. These can also be noisy, and heat up the space, and are not small and convenient; however, if you are someone looking for convenience, then this is the Air Fryer to go for.

ACCESSORY TOOLS FOR AIR FRYER COOKING

I love how Air Fryers save time, so I've compiled a list of my favourite time-saving tools that I often use when meal prepping with my Air Fryer. Anything to help make your life easier and healthier should certainly be considered, and what better way to help than by adding some accessories to your Air Fryer inventory?

MANDOLINE

Preparation is always needed before jumping into air frying, and getting yourself the mandoline slicer is the perfect tool to slice online rings, pickles, or even the best and crunchiest chips. You can select the thickness or thinness, depending on what the recipe needs and says, so you will always be able to get the perfect crispness.

GRILL PAN

This is simply a pan created with a perforated surface. With this tool, you can both grill and sear foods like fish or even vegetables inside your Air Fryer. They are also commonly non-stick, which really helps your overall clean-up.

However, before you purchase a grill pan, make sure the Air Fryer model you have does support the grill pan. The last thing you want is to find that your grill pan just does not fit inside your Air Fryer.

HEAT RESISTANT TONGS

There is no denying how hot an Air Fryer can get inside, and unless you are a superhero, you will need some help manoeuvring in foods in and outside of the basket if need be. Using heat-resistant tongs can really make your life infinitely easier by keeping your foods, and your hands, safe. They are affordable, and really useful to allow for an even cooking process.

AIR FRYER LINERS

If you'd like to further decrease your clean-up time, then this is for you! These liners are both non-stick and non-toxic, making this a classic little investment for you to consider. They prevent the food from sticking to your Air Fryer and help in the process of keeping your little machine clean. You will not have to worry about burnt foods inside your fryer again!

AIR FRYER RACK

This adds a little bit more versatility as you can really take advantage of the surface cooking. With a rack, you ensure that heat is evenly distributed to all 360 degrees of your food. They are very safe and easy to use, and they increase the number of dishes you can cook at the same time

BAKING PANS

With an Air Fryer, you can even bake! You just need the right equipment, such as a barrel or round pan. With this you can even bake pizza, bread, muffins, and more. Imagine telling people you baked your own cake with an Air Fryer!

SILICONE BAKING CUPS

From egg bites to muffins, these are individual cups you can use in order to help compensate for the smaller space within an Air Fryer. The silicone material is heat-resistant, and allows for easier release of the contents, which spares you a lot of time cleaning. If you are a fan of baking, then this is a must have.

OIL SPRAYER

Naturally, one of the top benefits is needing much less oil when cooking with an Air Fryer, but it does not necessarily mean that you can cook with no oil at all. An oil sprayer is the key to getting the food you want to that nice golden-brown. You can use any oil that you like to use when cooking; all you need is a little spritz before you close the machine, and you are set!

THERMAPEN

Having the right cooking time is very important, but temperature also counts for a lot, and this is a nice little accessory to add to your collection. Having an instant-read thermometer can ensure all the food you have is cooked (and evenly so). If you are not completely certain at what temperatures food should be, you can always check out the various different guides.

HOW TO CLEAN AN AIR FRYER

As mentioned before, an Air Fryer is really easy to clean, but that doesn't mean you'll never need to clean it! Also, please remember that the cleanliness of your machine depends on how often you use it, and what you use it for.

It is recommended that you clean your Air Fryer after every use. As tempting as it may be to skip a day, it really is not worth it over the long run.
And that is the first step that comes with cleaning an Air Fryer:

- Do not delay the cleaning. Simply don't. Allowing crumbs or random bits of food to harden overnight can turn an easy task into a nightmare of a chore. If you do happen to air-fry foods that come with a form of sticky sauce, then the warmer they are, the easier again they will be to clean and remove.

- Unplug the machine, and use warm and soapy water to properly remove the dirt and components. You do not want anything abrasive in there. If there is food that gets stuck, try soaking it until it is soft enough to remove.

- If there is any food that happens to be stuck on the grate or in the basket, then you should consider gently using a toothpick or even a wooden skewer to scrape it off, in order to be thorough with your cleaning process.

- Remember to wipe the inside with a damp, soapy cloth, and remember to remove both the drawer and the basket.

- Finally, wipe the outside of your Air Fryer with a damp cloth or a sponge.

If there are any odors that seem to be stuck to your Air Fryer after cooking a strong food, even after you have cleaned it, then you can consider using a product called NewAir.

Just soak it in with water for about 3o minutes to an hour before you clean it. If the smell remains, then rub one lemon half over the drawer and the basket. Allow it to soak for another 30 minutes before washing it again.

Please do be careful with any non-stick appliances. They are a wonder for cleaning, but they can flake or come off over time. Be gentle, as you do not want anything to scratch or to even chip the coating. Not only does it ruin a little bit of the aesthetic look, a small part of your Air Fryer will constantly be struggling with sticky food.

There you have it! The first stepping stones and foundational knowledge of an Air Fryer. The device you will choose, and how you will use it is up to you, but there are still so many exciting varieties, choices, and options to come!

SWEET POTATO HASH

15 minutes

45 minutes

3

INGREDIENTS

- 2 sweet potatoes, cubed
- 2 slices of bacon, small cubes
- 2 tbsp. olive oil
- 1 tbsp. smoked paprika
- 1 tsp. salt
- 1 tsp. black pepper (ground)
- 1 tsp. dill weed (dried)

DIRECTIONS

1. Preheat your Air Fryer to 200°C
2. Take a large bowl and add the olive oil
3. Add the potatoes, bacon, salt, pepper, dill, and paprika into the bowl and toss to evenly coat
4. Pour now the contents of the bowl into your Air Fryer and cook for 12-16 minutes, stir halfway through.
5. Serve.

Nutrition: Calories: 152; Fat: 6 g; Protein: 3.5 g; Carbs: 21.5 g; Fibre: 2.5 g; Sugar: 1 g

EGG & HAM CUPS

14 minutes

20 minutes

4

INGREDIENTS

- 4 eggs
- 8 slices of bread, pre-toasted
- 2 slices of ham
- A pinch of salt
- A pinch of pepper
- A little extra butter for greasing

DIRECTIONS

1. Take 4 ramekins and brush them with butter to grease the inside
2. Take the slices of bread and flatten them down with a rolling pin
3. Arrange the toast inside the ramekins, rolling it around the sides, with 2 slices in each ramekin
4. Line the inside of each ramekin with a slice of ham
5. Crack one egg into each ramekin
6. Season with a little salt and pepper
7. Place now the ramekins into your Air Fryer and cook at 160°C for 15 minutes
8. Remove from the fryer and wait to cool just slightly
9. Remove from the ramekins and serve

Nutrition: Calories: 204; Fat: 6 g; Protein: 12 g; Carbs: 24 g; Fibre: 5 g; Sugar: 3 g

AIR FRYER BOILED EGGS

1 minutes

10 minutes

4

INGREDIENTS

- 4 eggs (use as many as you want)

DIRECTIONS

1. Place room temperature eggs in the basket of the air fryer, leaving space between the eggs to allow the hot air to circulate.Use a metal rack to fit more, if necessary.
2. Set the air fryer to 150°C. Cook according your preferences (from 8 minutes for soft-boiled eggs to 12 minutes for hard-boiled eggs).
3. Once cooked, remove from the airfryer basket and place in an ice bath or bowl of cold water. This will prevent the eggs from continuing to cook. When it's cool and safe to touch, remove the skin.

Nutrition: Calories: 72; Fat: 5g; Carbohydrates: 0g; Fibre: 0g; Sugar: 0g; Protein: 6g

FRIED BACON

10 minutes

10 minutes

2

INGREDIENTS

- 4-5 rashers of lean bacon, fat cut off

DIRECTIONS

1. Line up the Air Fryer basket with parchment paper, to soak up excess grease
2. Arrange your bacon in the basket, ensuring you don't overcrowd; around 4-5 slices should be enough, depending upon the size of your machine
3. Set the fryer to 200°C
4. Cook for 10 minutes for crispy, and an extra 2 if you want it super-crispy
5. Serve and enjoy!

Nutrition: Calories: 161; Fat: 12 g; Protein: 12 g; Carbs: 0.5 g; Fibre: 0 g; Sugar: 0 g

SAUSAGES IN AIR FRYER

5 minutes

12 minutes

6

INGREDIENTS

- 6 Sausages
- 3 squirts Spray Oil

DIRECTIONS

1. Preheat your air fryer to 180°C for 5 minutes
2. Prick each sausage a couple of times (you can use a knife or fork).
3. Spray the bottom of the air fryer with a few splashes of oil to prevent the sausages from sticking.
4. Use the tongs to gently insert the sausages (do not let them touch so that they cook evenly).
5. Set timer to 12 minutes (adjust the time for small, large or frozen sausages).
6. Halfway through cooking, turn with tongs.
7. Check after 12 minutes and reheat if necessary.Serve with your chosen meal

Nutrition: Calories: 209kcal; Carbohydrates: 2g; Protein: 11g; Fat: 17g

AIR FRYER BLACK PUDDING(PACKED)

0 minutes

9 minutes

2

INGREDIENTS

- Black Pudding Slices

DIRECTIONS

1. If your black pudding is still frozen, air fry it in the air fryer for 6 minutes at 80°C, then it will be soft enough to cut.
2. Remove from the air fryer. Cut into slices, removing the wrapper.
3. Place the slices in the frying basket and cook at 180°C for 9 minutes.
4. Serve.

Nutrition: Calories: 297kcal; Fat: 22 g

BACON MUFFINS

7 minutes

6 minutes

1

INGREDIENTS

- 1 Large Egg
- 1 Slice of Unsmoked Bacon
- 1 English All Butter Muffin
- 2 Slices of Burger Cheese
- 1 Pinch of Salt and Pepper

DIRECTIONS

1. Crack the large egg into either a ramekin or oven proof dish
2. Slice the muffin in half
3. Layer 1 slice of burger cheese on 1 half
4. Place now the muffin and bacon in the Air Fryer drawer, place the ovenproof dish or ramekin in the drawer too.
5. Heat up the Air Fryer to 200°C for 6 minutes
6. Once is done, assemble the breakfast muffin and add the extra slice of cheese on top.

Nutrition: Calories: 291; Fat: 12 g; Protein: 15 g; Carbs: 25 g; Fibre: 2 g; Sugar: 0 g

CHOCOLATE CHIP COOKIES

10 minutes

15 minutes

12

INGREDIENTS

- 115 g butter, melted
- 55 g brown sugar
- 50 g caster sugar
- 1 large egg
- 1 tsp. pure vanilla extract
- 185 g plain flour
- 1/2 tsp. bicarbonate of soda
- 1/2 tsp. salt
- 120 g chocolate chips
- 35 g chopped walnuts

DIRECTIONS

1. Take medium bowl and whisk together melted butter and sugars.
2. Add egg and vanilla, whisk until incorporated.
3. Add salt, flour, bicarbonate of soda and stir.
4. Arrange a small piece of parchment in the Air Fryer's basket, making sure there is air flow around the edges.
5. Work in batches, using a large cookie scoop and scoop dough onto parchment, about 3 tablespoons, leaving 5cm between each of them, press to flatten slightly.
6. Bake in the Air Fryer at 180°C for 8 minutes. Cookies will be golden and slightly soft. Let them cool 5 minutes before serving.

Nutrition: Calories: 224; Fat: 13 g; Protein: 3.5 g; Carbs: 24 g; Fibre: 2 g; Sugar: 12 g

VEGETABLE FRITTATA

5 minutes

10 minutes

1 Frittata

INGREDIENTS

- Oil or butter to grease the pan
- 3 eggs
- 1/4 red pepper, diced
- 1/4 green pepper, diced
- 10 baby spinach leaves, chopped
- Handful of cheddar cheese, grated
- Salt and pepper to season, optional

DIRECTIONS

1. Take a bowl and beat the eggs inside. Season with salt and pepper (optional).
2. Grease the pan with the oil or butter and place it in the Air Fryer. Switch to 180°C, allow to heat up for a minute. Add the peppers, cook for 3 minutes.
3. Pour the spinach and egg mix in. Sprinkle grated cheese across the top. Cook for another 6 minutes, checking to make sure it isn't over cooking.

Nutrition: Calories: 514; Fat: 31 g; Protein: 38 g; Carbs: 18 g; Fibre: 8 g; Sugar: 3 g

SAUSAGE SANDWICHES

11 minutes

15 minutes

4

INGREDIENTS

- 4 breakfast sausage patties
- 4 eggs
- kosher salt, pepper
- 1 tbsp. butter
- 4 bagel thins or english muffins
- 4 slices cheese of choice

DIRECTIONS

1. Lay the breakfast sausage patties in your Air Fryer basket. Set the Air Fryer to 200°C, 15 minutes.
2. Remove the sausage and lay on some paper towels to drain the excess fat.
3. Take a bowl and beat the eggs inside, add kosher salt and pepper. In a medium size skillet, medium low heat, add butter, once it's melted add beaten eggs in a single layer.
4. Cook 2-3 minutes and flip, cook one or two more minutes. Remove the eggs from the pan, cut into 4 equal pieces.
5. Lay the bottom part of the English muffin or the bagel in the Air Fryer basket. Add a sausage patty to each, top with the cooked egg and a slice of cheese.
6. Put the top of the english muffin or the bagel on each sandwich.
7. Set the Air Fryer to 200°C, 4 to 5 minutes.
8. Serve.

Nutrition: Calories: 323; Fat: 13 g; Protein: 22 g; Carbs: 29 g; Fibre: 4 g; Sugar: 1 g

CHEESE OMELETTE

10 minutes

10 minutes

1

INGREDIENTS

- 2 eggs
- 150 ml milk
- Pinch of salt
- 40g shredded cheese
- Any toppings you like, such as mushrooms, peppers, onions, etc

DIRECTIONS

1. In a medium mixing jug, combine the eggs and milk
2. Add the salt and garnishes and combine well
3. Take a 15x8 cm pan and grease well, before pouring the mixture inside
4. Arrange the pan inside the Air Fryer basket
5. Cook at 170°C for 10 minutes
6. At the halfway point, sprinkle the cheese on top and loosen the edges with a spatula
7. Remove and enjoy!

Nutrition: Calories: 395; Fat: 27 g; Protein: 25 g; Carbs: 7 g; Fibre: 0 g; Sugar: 6 g

SCOTCH EGGS

15 minutes

12 minutes

6

INGREDIENTS

- 6 boiled eggs peeled
- 1 packet 400g Powters Sausagemeat
- 30 g Flour
- ½ teaspoon garlic powder
- 1 large egg beaten
- 120 g Breadcrumbs
- 1 tablespoon brown sugar
- ½ smoked paprika

DIRECTIONS

1. Divide the sausage into 6 equal portions and roll them into a balls
2. Place a sausage ball on your counter or parchment paper if you don't want to clean up later.
3. Pat the sausage balls until they reach the form of an oval big enough to hold an egg.
4. Place the peeled, boiled eggs in the center of the sausages patties and wrap the sausages around the eggs, applying pressure with your hands.
5. Now take 3 bowls and put, in order: flour and garlic powder combined, beaten egg, panko or breadcrumbs with brown sugar and smoked paprika.
6. Roll each sausage-covered egg in bowl 1, then dip in bowl 2 and coat in the breadcrumbs bowl.
7. Preheat your air fryer to 190°C for 10 minutes.
8. Place Scotch eggs in the air fryer basket, ensuring enough space between each other to let the air circulate.
9. Air fry the eggs for 12 minutes, evenly turning halfway through to brown.

Nutrition: Calories 396; Fat 27 g; Protein 29 g; Carbs 16 g; Fiber 1 g; Sugar 1 g

CHAPTER 2: POULTRY RECIPES

CHICKEN WINGS WITH HONEY AND SESAME

< 30 minutes

10-30 minutes

1-2

INGREDIENTS

- 450–500g **chicken wings** with tips removed
- 1 tbsp. **olive oil**
- 3 tbsp. **cornflour**
- 1 tbsp. runny **honey**
- 1 tsp. **soy sauce** or tamari
- 1 tsp. **rice wine** vinegar
- 1 tsp. toasted **sesame oil**
- 2 tsp. **sesame seeds**, toasted
- 1 large **spring onion**, thinly sliced
- salt and freshly ground **black pepper**

DIRECTIONS

1. Take a large bowl, toss together chicken wings, olive oil and a generous amount of salt and black pepper.
2. Toss in the cornflour, one tablespoon at a time, until the wings are well coated.
3. Air-fry the chicken wings in a single layer for 25 minutes, 180°C, turning halfway through.
4. Meanwhile, in a large bowl, make the glaze by whisking together the soy sauce, honey, rice, wine vinegar and toasted sesame oil.
5. Now tip the cooked wings into the glaze, tossing until coated. Place them in the Air Fryer in a single layer for another 5 minutes.
6. Toss the wings in the remaining glaze. Now sprinkle with the toasted sesame seeds and the spring onion.
7. Serve.

Nutrition: Calories: 544; Fat: 32.5 g; Protein: 37.5g; Carbs: 23.5 g; Fibre: 2 g; Sugar: 9 g

CHICKEN TENDERS

10 minutes

20 minutes

4

INGREDIENTS

For The Chicken Tenders:
- 675 g chicken tenders
- Salt
- Freshly ground black pepper
- 195 g plain flour
- 250 g panko breadcrumbs
- 2 large eggs
- 60 ml buttermilk
- Cooking spray

For The Honey Mustard:
- 80 g mayonnaise
- 3 tbsp. honey
- 2 tbsp. dijon mustard
- 1/4 tsp. hot sauce (optional)
- Pinch of salt
- Freshly ground black pepperw

DIRECTIONS

1. Season the chicken tenders with some salt and some black pepper on both sides. Place flour, breadcrumbs in two separate shallow bowls. Whisk eggs and buttermilk in a third bowl. Dip chicken in flour, one at a time, then egg mixture, and in breadcrumbs, pressing to coat.
2. Place the chicken tenders in your Air Fryer basket, do not overcrowd it. Spray the tops with cooking spray, cook at 200°C, 5 minutes. Flip the chicken over, spray the tops with more cooking spray, cook another 5 minutes. Repeat with the remaining chicken tenders.
3. Make the sauce: Take a small bowl, whisk together honey, mayonnaise, dijon, and hot sauce (optional). Add salt and a few cracks of black pepper.
4. Serve with honey mustard.

Nutrition: Calories: 720; Fat: 21 g; Protein: 55 g; Carbs: 74 g; Fibre: 7 g; Sugar: 11 g

ROTISSERIE CHICKEN

10 minutes

40 minutes

6

INGREDIENTS

- 2 tsp. of onion powder
- 1 tsp. of smoked paprika
- 1/4 tsp. of cayenne
- 1 (1.3kg.) chicken, into 8 pieces
- 2 tsp. of dried oregano
- Salt
- 2 tsp. of garlic powder
- Freshly ground black pepper
- 1 tbsp. of dried thyme

DIRECTIONS

1. Season all the chicken with salt and pepper. Take a medium bowl, whisk together herbs and spices, then rub the spice mix all over the chicken.
2. Add dark meat pieces to the Air Fryer basket and cook at 180°C, 10 minutes, then flip, cook 10 minutes more. Repeat with the chicken breasts, but reducing time to 16 minutes, 8 per side. Using a meat thermometer, check that the chicken is cooked through, each piece should register 73°C.

Nutrition: Calories: 200; Fat: 5 g; Protein: 35.5 g; Carbs: 0 g; Fibre: 0 g; Sugar: 0 g

CHICKEN NUGGETS

20 minutes

10 minutes

4

INGREDIENTS

- 500g chicken tenders
- 4 tbsp. salad dressing mix
- 2 tbsp. plain flour
- 1 egg, beaten
- 50g dry breadcrumbs

DIRECTIONS

1. Take a large mixing bowl and add the chicken
2. Sprinkle the seasoning over the top and ensure the chicken is evenly coated
3. Allow the chicken to rest for 10 minutes
4. Add the flour into a resealable bag
5. Pour the breadcrumbs onto a medium sized plate
6. Transfer the chicken into the resealable bag and coat with the flour, giving it a good shake
7. Remove the chicken and dip into the egg, and then roll into the breadcrumbs, coating evenly
8. Repeat with the chicken
9. Heat your Air Fryer to 200°C
10. Arrange the chicken inside the fryer and cook for 4 minutes, before turning over and cooking for another 4 minutes
11. Remove and serve whilst hot

Nutrition: Calories: 291.5; Fat: 13 g; Protein: 29 g; Carbs: 11 g; Fibre: 1 g; Sugar: 0.5 g

CHICKEN STRIPS

< 30 minutes

10-30 minutes

3

INGREDIENTS

- 2 large garlic cloves, minced or crushed
- 5 tbsp. plain yogurt
- ¼ tsp. salt, plus extra for seasoning
- 2 chicken breasts
- 6 tbsp. plain flour
- 6 tbsp. panko breadcrumbs
- 1 tsp. sweet smoked paprika
- 1 tsp. garlic granules
- ½ tsp. cayenne pepper
- freshly ground black pepper
- 1 free-range egg
- olive oil cooking spray

For the creamy honey mustard dip:

- 1 tbsp. runny honey
- 1 tbsp. light mayonnaise
- 1 tbsp. Dijon mustard
- ½ tbsp. wholegrain mustard
- ½ tsp. white wine vinegar

DIRECTIONS

1. To marinate the chicken, mix garlic, yoghurt and salt. Cut the chicken into 3cm wide strips, marinate in the yoghurt mixture for 20 minutes or more.
2. Take a medium bowl and mix the flour, paprika, breadcrumbs, cayenne pepper, garlic granules and a good amount of salt and pepper to create dredging mixture. Take another small bowl, beat the egg and add salt, pepper.
3. Shake off any excess yogurt from each of the chicken strip before dipping it first in the egg, then in the dredging mixture. Use different hands for wet and dry ingredients.
4. Spray the bottom of the Air Fryer basket with olive oil spray, arrange a single layer of chicken strips in the bottom. Spray the top of the strips with oil before air-frying 15 minutes, 200°C, turning roughly halfway through. Repeat until all the strips are cooked (work in batches).
5. Meanwhile, mix all the ingredients for the creamy honey mustard dip in a small bowl, set aside.
6. Serve.

Nutrition: Calories: 452; Fat: 15.5 g; Protein: 36 g; Carbs: 38 g; Fibre: 3 g; Sugar: 2.5 g

TURKEY AND MUSHROOM BURGERS

10 minutes

10 minutes

2

INGREDIENTS

- 180g mushrooms
- 500g minced turkey
- 1 tsp. garlic powder
- 1 tsp. onion powder
- ½ tsp. salt
- ½ tsp. pepper

DIRECTIONS

1. Take your food processor and add the mushrooms, pulsing into they form a puree. Season and pulse once more
2. Remove from the food processor and tip into a mixing bowl
3. Add the turkey to the bowl and combine well
4. Take a little of the mixture into your hands and shape into burgers. You should be able to make five
5. Spray each burger with a little cooking spray and place in the Air Fryer
6. Cook at 160°C for 10 minutes

Nutrition: Calories: 357.5; Fat: 14 g; Protein: 54 g; Carbs: 0 g; Fibre: 0 g; Sugar: 0 g

GARLIC HERB TURKEY BREAST

5 minutes

45 minutes

6

INGREDIENTS

- 900 g turkey breast, skin on
- Salt
- 1 tsp. freshly chopped rosemary
- Freshly ground black pepper
- 1 tsp. freshly chopped thyme
- 4 tbsp. butter, melted
- 3 cloves garlic, crushed

DIRECTIONS

1. Pat the turkey breast dry and add salt and pepper on both sides.
2. Take a small bowl, mix melted butter, garlic, thyme, and rosemary.
3. Brush the butter all over the turkey breast.
4. Arrange in your Air Fryer basket, skin side up, cook at 190°C (170°C fan), 40 minutes, until internal temperature reaches 73°C, flip halfway through.
5. Let it rest for 5 minutes before slicing.

Nutrition: Calories: 328; Fat: 18 g; Protein: 33 g; Carbs: 5.5 g; Fibre: 0.5 g; Sugar: 0 g

CHICKEN BREAST

5 minutes

15 minutes

2

INGREDIENTS

- Wax paper or plastic wrap
- 2 skinless/boneless chicken breast halves
- 1 tsp. salt
- 2 tsp. paprika
- 2 tsp. onion powder
- 2 tsp. black pepper
- 1 tsp. white pepper
- 1 tsp. cayenne pepper
- 1 tsp. ground cumin
- 1 tsp. ground oregano

DIRECTIONS

1. Put your chicken breasts between a few sheets of wax paper or plastic wrap and use a meat pounder until the chicken is evenly thick.
2. Make the blackened seasoning by mixing paprika, salt, onion powder, the 3 types of pepper, ground cumin, ground oregano. Check that the spices are well mixed.
3. Dredge the chicken in the seasoning spice mixture.
4. Place the chicken breasts in the Air Fryer basket. Temperature to 145°C, cook for 8 minutes.
5. After 8 minutes, remove the basket, turn the chicken breasts over. Set the temperature to 180°C and cook for 6 more minutes.

Nutrition: Calories: 355.5; Fat: 18.5 g; Protein: 41.5 g; Carbs: 1 g; Fibre: 0 g; Sugar: 0 g

CHICKEN THIGHS IN AIR FRYER

5 minutes

25 minutes

4-5

INGREDIENTS

- 1 kg chicken thighs
- 2 tsp your Seasoning of choice (Piri Piri, Curry, Garlic, Chili etc…)

DIRECTIONS

1. Preheat tyour air fryer to 200 °C. Lightly clean the chicken legs with kitchen paper before seasoning them.
2. Place the seasoned chicken legs in the air fryer. Depending on the size of your air fryer, you may have to do this in batches or use a trivet or rack if possible.
3. Cook for 10 minutes before turning the thighs over. Cook for a further 10 minutes. They should be crispy and fully cooked - if not, put them back in the air fryer for another 5 minutes or until cooked through.Internal temperature should be 75C.
4. Enjoy them with your favourite side dish!

Nutrition: Calories: 552; Fat: 41.5 g; Protein: 41 g; Carbs: 0 g; Fibre: 0 g; Sugar: 0 g

CHICKEN PARMESAN

16 minutes

10 minutes

4

INGREDIENTS

- 1/2 tsp. garlic powder
- 1/2 tsp. chilli flakes
- 240 g marinara/tomato sauce
- 100 g grated mozzarella
- Freshly chopped parsley, for garnish
- 2 large boneless chicken breasts
- Salt
- 100 g panko breadcrumbs
- 25 g freshly grated Parmesan
- 1 tsp. dried oregano
- Freshly ground black pepper
- 40 g plain flour
- 2 large eggs

DIRECTIONS

1. Cut the chicken to create 4 thin pieces. Add salt and pepper on both sides.
2. Prepare dredging station: Place the flour in a shallow bowl, add a large pinch of salt and pepper. Now place the eggs in a second bowl and beat them. Take a third bowl, mix Parmesan, breadcrumbs, garlic powder, oregano and chilli flakes.
3. One at a time, coat in flour, then dip in eggs, and finally press both sides into your panko mixture.
4. Arrange the chicken into your Air Fryer basket and cook 5 minutes on each side, 200°C. Top the chicken with sauce, mozzarella and cook 3 minutes more, 200°C, until cheese is melty and golden.
5. Serve with parsley garnish.

Nutrition: Calories: 397; Fat: 18 g; Protein: 30 g; Carbs: 25 g; Fibre: 2.5 g; Sugar: 5 g

BEEF FRIED RICE

10 minutes

15 minutes

3

INGREDIENTS

- 100 g cooked rice
- 500 g beef strips, cooked
- 1 tbsp. sesame oil
- 1 onion, diced
- 1 egg
- 2 tsp. garlic powder
- 1 tbsp. vegetable oil
- 100 g frozen peas
- Salt
- Pepper
-

DIRECTIONS

1. Preheat Air Fryer to 175°C
2. Add pepper, salt and garlic powder to the beef
3. Cook the beef in a pan until almost done
4. Mix the rice with peas, carrots and vegetable oil, combining well
5. Add the rice mixture to the beef and combine
6. Add to the Air Fryer and cook for about 10 minutes
7. Add the egg and cook until the egg has completely cooked

Nutrition: Calories: 446; Fat: 14 g; Protein: 44 g; Carbs: 31 g; Fibre: 2 g; Sugar: 2 g

HERBED STEAK

30 minutes

20 minutes

4

INGREDIENTS

- 4 tbsp. butter, softened
- 2 cloves garlic, crushed
- 2 tsp. freshly chopped parsley
- 1 tsp. freshly chopped chives
- 1 tsp. freshly chopped thyme
- 1 tsp. freshly chopped rosemary
- 1 (900g) bone-in ribeye
- Salt
- Freshly ground black pepper

DIRECTIONS

1. In a small bowl, mix butter, herbs. Arrange in centre of a piece of cling film and roll into a log. Twist ends together to keep tight and refrigerate until hardened, 20 minutes.
2. Add salt and pepper on both sides of the steak.
3. Place steak in the Air Fryer basket and cook, flipping halfway through, 200°C 12-14 minutes for medium, depending on thickness of steak.
4. Top your steak with a slice of herb butter.

Nutrition: Calories: 415; Fat: 22 g; Protein: 51 g; Carbs: 3 g; Fibre: 0 g; Sugar: 0 g

MOZZARELLA-STUFFED MEATBALLS

15 minutes

15 minutes

4

INGREDIENTS

- 450 g beef mince
- 50 g breadcrumbs
- 25 g freshly grated Parmesan
- 5 g freshly chopped parsley
- 1 large egg
- 2 cloves garlic, crushed
- 1 tsp. dried oregano
- Salt
- Freshly ground black pepper
- 85 g fresh mozzarella, cut into 16 cubes
- Marinara, for serving

DIRECTIONS

1. Take a large bowl, mix beef, parsley, breadcrumbs, Parmesan, egg, garlic, oregano. Add salt and pepper.
2. Scoop 2 tablespoons of meat, flatten into a patty in your hand. Arrange a cube of mozzarella in the centre and pinch the meat up around the cheese and roll into a ball. Repeat with remaining meat to make 16 total meatballs.
3. Arrange the meatballs in the Air Fryer basket and cook 190°C, 12 minutes.
4. Serve with warmed marinara.

Nutrition: Calories: 363; Fat: 21.5 g; Protein: 30.5 g; Carbs: 7 g; Fibre: 0 g; Sugar: 0.5 g

BEEF KEBOBS

45 minutes

15 minutes

4

INGREDIENTS

- 500g beef, cubed
- 200g low fat sour cream
- 2 tbsp. soy sauce
- 1 bell pepper
- ½ onion, chopped
- 20 x 16 cm skewers

DIRECTIONS

1. Take a medium bowl and combine the sour cream and soy sauce
2. Add the cubed beef and marinate for at least 30 minutes
3. Cut the pepper and onion into 2.5 cm pieces
4. Soak the skewers in warm water for about 10 minutes
5. Place the beef, bell peppers and onion onto the skewers, alternating between each one
6. Cook at 200°C for 10 minutes, flip halfway through.

Nutrition: Calories: 250; Fat: 15 g; Protein: 23g ; Carbs: 4 g; Fibre: 0 g; Sugar: 0 g

PORK CHOPS

10 minutes

10 minutes

4

INGREDIENTS

- 4 boneless pork chops
- 2 tbsp. extra-virgin olive oil
- 50 g freshly grated Parmesan
- 1 tsp. salt
- 1 tsp. paprika
- 1 tsp. garlic powder
- 1 tsp. onion powder
- 1/2 tsp. freshly ground black pepper

DIRECTIONS

1. Pat your pork chops dry with some paper towels, then coat both of the sides with oil. Take a medium bowl, mix Parmesan, spices. Coat both of the sides of the pork chops with the Parmesan mixture.
2. Place the pork chops in Air Fryer basket, cook at 190°C for 9 minutes, flipping halfway through.

Nutrition: Calories: 306; Fat: 22 g; Protein: 23 g; Carbs: 1.5 g; Fibre: 0 g; Sugar: 0 g

MUSTARD GLAZED PORK

2 hours

20 minutes

4

INGREDIENTS

- 750 g pork tenderloin
- 1 tbsp. minced garlic
- ¼ tsp. salt
- Pinch of cracked black pepper
- 3 tbsp. mustard
- 3 tbsp. brown sugar
- 1 tsp. Italian seasoning
- 1 tsp. rosemary

DIRECTIONS

1. Cut slits into the pork and place the minced garlic into the slits.
2. Season with the salt and pepper.
3. Take a mixing bowl and add the remaining ingredients, combining well.
4. Rub the mix over the pork and allow to marinate for 2 hours.
5. Place in the Air Fryer and cook at 200°C for 20 minutes.

Nutrition: Calories: 256; Fat: 5.5 g; Protein: 23 g; Carbs: 8.5 g; Fibre: 0.5 g; Sugar: 7.5 g

LAMB STEAKS

5 minutes

10 minutes

4

INGREDIENTS

- 4 Lamb Steaks
- 1 tsp. Frozen Chopped Garlic
- 2 tsp. **Extra Virgin Olive Oil**
- 2 tsp. Lemon Juice
- 2 tsp. **Honey**
- 1 tsp. **Thyme**
- Salt & Pepper
- Fresh Mint

DIRECTIONS

1. Place the lamb steaks on a chopping board, season with salt, pepper and dried thyme.
2. Thinly chop two tablespoons of mint and load into a bowl with everything except the lamb. Mix well then spoon over the lamb steaks. Place the steaks into the fridge for an hour, allow to marinate.
3. Load the steaks into the Air Fryer basket, add extra mint.
4. Air fry 10 minutes, 180°C.

Nutrition: Calories: 274.5; Fat: 19 g; Protein: 21g; Carbs: 4 g; Fibre: 0 g; Sugar: 4 g

ROAST BEEF

5 minutes

35 minutes

8

INGREDIENTS

- 1 Kg Beef Roast (up to 1.5 Kg)
- 1 tbsp Olive Oil
- Seasoning to taste

DIRECTIONS

1. Tie the roast to make it more compact
2. Rub the roast with oil
3. Add any seasonings you like
4. Place the beef in the air fryer basket
5. Air fry at 180°C for about 15 minutes per half of Kg (for medium rare beef).
6. Let the roast rest for 5 minutes and serve

Notes

Rare: 46 to 49°C (50 final temperature)

Medium-Rare: 50 to 55°C (58 final temperature)

Medium: 58 to 60°C (63 final temperature)

Medium-Well: 60 to 63°F (65 final temperature)

Well-Done: 65 to 69°F (72 final temperature)

Nutrition: Calories: 443; Fat: 29 g; Carbohydrates: 0 g; Fiber: 0 g; Sugar: 0 g; Protein: 43 g

SIMPLE HAMBURGERS

5 minutes

15 minutes

4

INGREDIENTS

- 500 g minced beef
- Salt
- Pepper

DIRECTIONS

1. Preheat Air Fryer to 200°C.
2. Divide minced beef into 4 equal portions and form them into burgers with your hands.
3. Season with salt, pepper, to your taste.
4. Air fry for 10 minutes.
5. Flip your burgers over, cook for a further 3 minutes.

Nutrition: Calories: 247.5; Fat: 15 g; Protein: 24 g; Carbs: 0 g; Fibre: 0 g; Sugar: 0 g

BEEF WELLINGTON

15 minutes

35 minutes

8

INGREDIENTS

- 1kg beef fillet (one large piece)
- Chicken pate
- 2 sheets of shortcrust pastry
- 1 egg, beaten
- Salt
- Pepper

DIRECTIONS

1. Season the beef with salt, pepper and wrap tightly in cling film
2. Place the beef in the refrigerator for at least one hour
3. Roll out the pastry and brush the edges with the beaten egg
4. Spread the pate over the pastry, making sure it is distributed equally
5. Take now the beef out of the refrigerator and remove the cling film
6. Place the beef in the middle of your pastry
7. Wrap your pastry around the meat and seal the edges with a fork
8. Place in the Air Fryer and cook at 160°C for 35 minutes

Nutrition: Calories: 509; Fat: 28 g; Protein: 34 g; Carbs: 28 g; Fibre: 1 g; Sugar: 0.5 g

SIMPLE SALMON

5 minutes

20-25 minutes

4

INGREDIENTS

- 4 salmon filets
- 3 lemons
- 8 sprigs rosemary
- 1 Tablespoon olive oil
- Salt

DIRECTIONS

1. Slice the lemons into thin slices.
2. Place several lemon slices on the bottom of the Air Fryer basket.
3. Now lay 4 rosemary sprigs on the lemons.
4. Arrange one salmon filet on top of each sprig of rosemary. Sprinkle some salt on the salmon.
5. Top each salmon filet with another sprig of rosemary. Cover with more lemon slices.
6. Drizzle with the olive oil on top.
7. Put the fry basket in the fryer. Set the temperature to 135°C. Set the timer for 20 minutes.
8. Take a fork and check the salmon, If it flakes easily, it's ready. If not, it needs 5 minutes more.
9. Serve the salmon with roasted lemon slices and rosemary.

Nutrition: Calories: 242; Fat: 12 g; Protein: 29 g; Carbs: 0 g; Fibre: 0 g; Sugar: 0 g

COCONUT PRAWNS

15 minutes

15 minutes

4

INGREDIENTS

For The Prawns:

- 450 g of large prawns, peeled, deveined, tails on
- Freshly ground black pepper
- 65 g of plain flour
- Salt
- 35 g of shredded sweetened coconut
- 2 large eggs, beaten
- 100 g of panko breadcrumbs

For The Dipping Sauce:

- 1 tbsp. of Sriracha
- 1 tbsp. of Thai sweet chilli sauce
- 120 g of mayonnaise

DIRECTIONS

1 Take a shallow bowl, add salt and pepper to flour. Take another shallow bowl, mix breadcrumbs and coconut. Arrange the eggs in a third shallow bowl.

2 Dip prawns in flour, then eggs, then coconut mixture, one at a time.

3 Arrange your prawns into the Air Fryer basket, heat to 200°C . Bake until the prawns are well golden and cooked through, 10-12 minutes.

4 Take a small bowl, mix Siracha, mayonnaise, chilli sauce.

5 Serve with dipping sauce.

Nutrition: Calories: 283; Fat: 6.5 g; Protein: 29 g; Carbs: 25 g; Fibre: 3 g; Sugar: 2 g

CRAB CAKES

20 minutes

15 minutes

4

INGREDIENTS

For The Crab Cakes:

- Cooking spray
- Hot sauce, for serving
- Lemon wedges, for serving
- 60 g of mayonnaise
- 1 egg
- 2 tsp. of cajun seasoning
- 1 tsp. of lemon zest
- 1/2 tsp. of salt
- 450 g of jumbo lump crab meat
- 120 g of Cracker crumbs (from about 20 crackers)
- 2 tbsp. of chives, finely chopped
- 2 tsp. of Dijon mustard

For The Tartar Sauce:

- 1/4 tsp. of Dijon mustard
- 1 tsp. of fresh dill, finely chopped
- 60 g of mayonnaise
- 80 g dill pickle, finely chopped
- 2 tsp. of capers, finely chopped
- 1 tsp. of fresh lemon juice
- 1 tbsp. of shallot, finely chopped

DIRECTIONS

1 Take a large bowl, whisk together egg, mayo, chives, Dijon mustard, lemon zest, cajun seasoning, and salt. Fold in crab meat and cracker crumbs.
2 Divide your mixture to form 8 patties.
3 Heat your Air Fryer to 190°C, spray the basket and the tops of your cakes with some cooking spray. Arrange the cakes into the basket in a single layer. Cook until crisp and deep golden brown, 12-14 minutes, flip halfway through.
4 Take a bowl and mix all of the tartar sauce ingredients.
5 Serve the cakes warm with lemon wedges, hot sauce and tartar sauce.

Nutrition: Calories: 265; Fat: 8 g; Protein: 24.5 g; Carbs: 21 g; Fibre: 1 g; Sugar: 0 g

TILAPIA FILLETS

10 minutes

10 minutes

2

INGREDIENTS

- 50g almond flour
- 2 fillets of tilapia fish
- 2 tbsp. melted butter
- 1 tsp. black pepper
- ½ tsp. salt
- 4 tbsp. mayonnaise
- A handful of almonds, sliced thinly

DIRECTIONS

1   Take a mixing bowl and add the butter, almond flour, pepper and salt, combining well
2   Take the fish and spread the mayonnaise on both sides
3   Cover the fillets in the almond flour mix
4   Spread one side of the fish with the sliced almonds
5   Spray your Air Fryer with a little amount of cooking spray.
6   Add the fish into the Air Fryer and cook at 160°C for 10 minutes

Nutrition: Calories: 500; Fat: 30.5 g; Protein: 33 g; Carbs: 25 g; Fibre: 7 g; Sugar: 1.5 g

FISH TACOS

14 minutes

10 minutes

4

INGREDIENTS

- 500g mahi fish, fresh
- 8 small tortillas
- 2 tsp. Cajun seasoning
- 4 tbsp. sour cream
- 2 tbsp. mayo
- ¼ tbsp. cayenne
- 2 tbsp. pepper sauce
- A little salt and pepper
- 1 tbsp. sriracha sauce
- 2 tbsp. lime juice

DIRECTIONS

1 Cut the fish into slices and season with salt
2 Mix the cayenne pepper and black pepper with the Cajun seasoning. Sprinkle onto fish
3 Brush pepper sauce on both sides of the fish
4 Set Air Fryer to 180°C and cook for 10 mins
5 Take a medium bowl and combine the mayonnaise, sour cream, lime juice, sriracha and cayenne pepper
6 Assemble tacos the tacos and serve!

Nutrition: Calories: 447; Fat: 13 g; Protein: 31 g; Carbs: 48 g; Fibre: 3 g; Sugar: 3.5 g

PEPPERY LEMON SHRIMP

10 minutes

10 minutes

2

INGREDIENTS

- 1 tbsp. olive oil
- 350g prepared shrimps, uncooked
- Juice of 1 lemon
- 1 tsp. pepper
- ¼ tsp. paprika
- ¼ tsp. garlic powder
- 1 lemon, sliced

DIRECTIONS

1 Preheat the fryer to 200°C
2 Take a medium size mixing bowl, mix the pepper, lemon juice, garlic powder, paprika and the olive oil together
3 Add the shrimp to the bowl and make sure they're well coated
4 Arrange the shrimp into the basket of the fryer
5 Cook for between 6-8 minutes, until firm and pink
6 Serve!

Nutrition: Calories: 208; Fat: 7 g; Protein: 35 g; Carbs: 0 g; Fibre: 0 g; Sugar: 0 g

COCONUT PRAWNS WITH SAUCE

 5 minutes

 12 minutes

 4

INGREDIENTS

For The Prawns

- 65 g plain flour
- Salt
- Freshly ground black pepper
- 100 g panko bread crumbs
- 35 g shredded sweetened coconut
- 2 large eggs, beaten
- 450 g large prawns, peeled and deveined, tails on

For The Dipping Sauce

- 120 g mayonnaise
- 1 tbsp. Sriracha
- 1 tbsp. Thai sweet chilli sauce

DIRECTIONS

1. In a shallow bowl, season the flour with salt and pepper. In another shallow bowl, mix the breadcrumbs and coconut. Place the eggs in a third shallow bowl.
2. Dip the prawns one by one in flour, then in eggs, then in coconut mixture.
3. Put the prawns in the frying basket and air fry to 200°C.
4. Cook until they are golden brown and cooked through, 10 to 12 minutes. Work in batches as needed.
5. In a small bowl, mix together the mayonnaise, sriracha, and chilli sauce. Serve prawns with the sauce.

Nutrition: Calories: 374; Fat: 16.5 g; Protein: 29 g; Carbs: 25 g; Fibre: 3 g; Sugar: 2 g

TUNA PATTIES

15 minutes

10 minutes

10

INGREDIENTS

- 425 g canned albacore tuna, drained or 454g fresh tuna, diced
- 2-3 large eggs
- zest of 1 medium lemon
- 1 tbsp. lemon juice
- 1/4 tsp of **Kosher salt** , or to taste
- 55 g of breadcrumbs
- 1/2 tsp dried herbs (oregano, dill, basil, thyme or any combo)
- fresh cracked black pepper
- 3 tbsp grated parmesan cheese
- 1 stalk celery, finely chopped
- Optional: tartar sauce, ranch, mayo, lemon slices
- 3 tbsp minced onion
- 1/2 tsp garlic powder

DIRECTIONS

1 Take a medium bowl, mix the lemon zest, eggs, lemon juice, breadcrumbs, celery, parmesan cheese, onion, dried herbs, garlic powder, salt, pepper. Now stir well. Gently fold in the tuna.

2 Take your Air Fryer perforated baking paper, lay it inside the base of the Air Fryer. Now lightly spray the paper. if not you don't have it spray at the base of the Air Fryer basket to make sure they do not stick.

3 Try to keep all patties same size and thickness. Scoop 1/4 cup of the mixture, shape into patties about 8 cm wide x 1.3 cm thick and lay them inside the basket. Makes about 10 patties.

4 If patties are too soft, chill them for 1 hour or until firm. Brush the top of the patties with oil. Air Fry 185°C, 10 minutes, flip halfway through. After you flip the patties, spray the tops again.

5 Serve with your sauce and lemon slices.

Nutrition: Calories: 102.2; Fat: 3.9 g; Protein: 12.5 g; Carbs: 2.7 g; Fibre: 0 g; Sugar: 0 g

FRIED COD

15 minutes

15 minutes

3

INGREDIENTS

- 1 (450g) cod, cut into 4 strips
- Salt
- Freshly ground black pepper
- 65 g plain flour
- 1 large egg, beaten
- 200 g panko breadcrumbs
- 1 tsp. Old Bay seasoning
- Lemon wedges, for serving
- Tartar sauce, for serving

DIRECTIONS

1 Pat the fish dry and add salt and pepper on both sides.

2 Arrange egg, flour, and panko in three shallow bowls. Add Old Bay to panko and toss. Coat fish into the flour, then into the egg, and finally into panko, press to coat, one at a time.

3 Arrange the fish into the Air Fryer basket, cook 10-12 minutes, 200°C, or until fish is golden and flakes easily with a fork, gently flip halfway through.

4 Serve with lemon wedges and tartar sauce.

Nutrition: Calories: 397; Fat: 4.5 g; Protein: 37 g; Carbs: 48 g; Fibre: 3.5 g; Sugar: 3.5 g

SRIRACHA WITH SALMON

35 minutes

15 minutes

2

INGREDIENTS

- 3 tbsp. sriracha
- 4 tbsp. honey
- 1 tbsp. soy sauce
- 500 g salmon fillets

DIRECTIONS

1 Take a medium bowl and add the honey, soy sauce and sriracha, combining well
2 Place the salmon into the sauce skin, with the skin facing upwards
3 Allow to marinade for 30 minutes
4 Spray the basket with some cooking spray.
5 Heat the Air Fryer to 200°C
6 Place the salmon into the Air Fryer skin side down and cook for 12 minutes
7 Serve!

Nutrition: Calories: 505; Fat: 15 g; Protein: 50 g; Carbs: 38.5 g; Fibre: 0.5 g; Sugar: 37.5 g

BAKED CRUNCHY COD

10 minutes

15 minutes

2

INGREDIENTS

- 2 pieces of cod cut into smaller portions (around five)
- 4 tbsp. of panko breadcrumbs
- 1 egg
- 1 egg white
- ½ tsp. onion powder
- ½ tsp. garlic salt
- A pinch of pepper
- ½ tsp. mixed herbs

DIRECTIONS

1 Heat Air Fryer to 220°C
2 Take a small bowl and mix the egg and then add the egg white and combine once more
3 Cover the top of the fish with the herb mixture
4 Dip each piece of fish into the egg and then cover in the panko breadcrumbs
5 Line Air Fryer basket with tin foil
6 Place the fish in Air Fryer and cook for about 15 minutes

Nutrition: Calories: 291; Fat: 4 g; Protein: 45 g; Carbs: 12 g; Fibre: 0.5 g; Sugar: 1 g

GARLIC CAULIFLOWER

10 minutes

15 minutes

2-3

INGREDIENTS

- 2 tbsp. ghee or butter, melted
- Freshly ground black pepper
- 1/2 tsp. garlic powder
- 1/4 tsp. turmeric
- Salt
- 1 small head of 114.5cut into small florets

DIRECTIONS

1. Take a small bowl and whisk turmeric, ghee, garlic powder. Place cauliflower in a large bowl, pour over the ghee mixture, toss to coat until all the florets are yellow. Add a good amount of salt and pepper.
2. Preheat your Air Fryer to 190°C, 3 minutes. Arrange the cauliflower in a single layer into the basket and cook, toss halfway through, until golden brown, 10-12 minutes.

Nutrition: Calories: 114.5; Fat: 11.5 g; Protein: 1 g; Carbs: 2.5 g; Fibre: 1 g; Sugar: 1 g

FRIED CHIPS

5 minutes

20 minutes

4

INGREDIENTS

- Salt
- 1 kg of potatoes, peeled, cut into 1cm batons
- Oil spray (vegetable or sunflower works best)
- Other optional seasoning
- Your favourite dip

DIRECTIONS

1 Preheat to 180°C. Rinse the chips in cold water then pat them dry.
2 Place the chips into the Air Fryer basket and spray with oil. Sprinkle them with salt and any other seasoning you want, then shake the basket.
3 Air fry for 20 minutes, shake the chips halfway through to ensure even cooking. After it finishes, if the chips are not well cooked, place them back inside for 5 minutes more and continue to do so until they are good to go.
4 Serve with your favourite dip.

Nutrition: Calories: 192.5; Fat: 0 g; Protein: 5 g; Carbs: 43.5 g; Fibre: 5 g; Sugar: 2 g

BROCCOLI WITH OIL

 5 minutes

 10 minutes

 4

INGREDIENTS

- 1 medium head broccoli, cut into florets
- 1 tbsp. extra-virgin olive oil
- 1 clove garlic, crushed
- Salt
- Freshly ground black pepper
- Pinch chilli flakes

DIRECTIONS

1. Take a large bowl, toss broccoli with garlic and oil. Season with salt, pepper, chilli flakes.
2. Arrange the broccoli in a single layer inside the basket. Cook 10 minutes 180°C, until tender and crisp. Repeat with the remaining part.

Nutrition: Calories: 81; Fat: 4 g; Protein: 4 g; Carbs: 10 g; Fibre: 4 g; Sugar: 3 g

COURGETTE STICKS

10 minutes

20 minutes

4

INGREDIENTS

- 2 medium courgettes, sliced into 1/2cm rounds
- 2 large eggs
- 90 g panko breadcrumbs
- 50 g cornmeal
- 35 g freshly grated 182
- 1 tsp. dried oregano
- 1/4 tsp. garlic powder
- Pinch chilli flakes
- Salt
- Freshly ground black pepper
- Marinara, for serving

DIRECTIONS

1 Arrange the courgette on a platter lined with paper towels and pat dry.

2 Arrange the beaten eggs in a shallow bowl. Take another shallow bowl, mix cornmeal, panko, oregano, Parmesan, garlic powder, and a large pinch of chilli flakes. Add salt and pepper.

3 One at a time, dip the courgette rounds into the egg, then into the panko mixture, press to coat.

4 Arrange the courgette in an even layer, cook at 200°C 18 minutes, flip halfway through.

5 Serve warm with marinara.

Nutrition: Calories: 182; Fat: 5 g; Protein: 6.6 g; Carbs: 22 g; Fibre: 1 g; Sugar: 2 g

MOZZARELLA STICKS

30-60 minutes

10-30 minutes

3-4

INGREDIENTS

- 400 g block **mozzarella** cucina
- 2 tbsp. **plain flour**
- 1 tsp. **garlic** granules
- 1 large free-range **egg**
- 40g **panko**
- **olive oil** cooking spray
- salt and freshly ground black pepper

DIRECTIONS

1. Cut the mozzarella into strips, roughly 1.5 cm wide, pat dry using some kitchen paper.
2. In a shallow dish, combine flour and garlic granules. Take another dish, beat the egg and add a good amount of salt and pepper. Now spread the breadcrumbs in a third dish.
3. Roll your mozzarella strips into the flour, then into the egg, then into the flour and into the egg again, to create double coating. Check that each piece is totally covered in the flour each time. Coat well in the panko breadcrumbs.
4. Freeze 30 minutes or more, until solid.
5. Spray the bottom of your Air Fryer basket with olive oil spray, place a single layer of mozzarella sticks at the bottom. Now spray the top of the mozzarella sticks with oil, air fry 10 minutes, 200°C. Now repeat until all your mozzarella sticks are cooked, keeping each batch warm, then serve immediately.

Nutrition: Calories: 369; Fat: 23.5 g; Protein: 25 g; Carbs: 12 g; Fibre: 1 g; Sugar: 2 g

ROAST POTATOES

< 30 minutes

30-60 minutes

2

INGREDIENTS

- 2 large **floury potatoes** (approximately 450g)
- **salt**, to taste
- 1 tbsp. **olive oil**

DIRECTIONS

1 Peel, quarter your potatoes, then boil them in a saucepan of salted water for 15 minutes (place them when the water is already boiling).
2 Now drain the potatoes, leave them to steam dry for a minute or two.
3 Toss with olive oil and a good amount of salt.
4 Air fry 30 minutes, 200°C, toss every 10 minutes.
5 Serve.

Nutrition: Calories: 232.5; Fat: 7 g; Protein: 4.5 g; Carbs: 39 g; Fibre: 4.5 g; Sugar: 1.5 g

FRIED PICKLES

10 minutes

10 minutes

3

INGREDIENTS

- 300 g dill pickle slices
- 1 egg, whisked with 1 tbsp. water
- 50 g breadcrumbs
- 25 g freshly grated Parmesan
- 1 tsp. dried oregano
- 1 tsp. garlic powder
- Ranch, for dipping

DIRECTIONS

1 Using paper towels, pat pickle chips dry. In a medium bowl, stir together breadcrumbs, Parmesan, oregano, and garlic powder.
2 Dredge pickle chips first in egg and then in the bread crumb mixture. Arrange a single layer into the Air Fryer basket. Cook at 200°C for 10 minutes.
3 Serve warm with ranch.

Nutrition: Calories: 115; Fat: 3.5 g; Protein: 6 g; Carbs: 11 g; Fibre: 1 g; Sugar: 2 g

AUBERGINE STICKS

9 minutes

15 minutes

4

INGREDIENTS

- 1 medium aubergine
- 1 tbsp. extra-virgin olive oil
- 1 tsp. dried oregano
- 1/2 tsp. garlic powder
- Salt
- Freshly ground black pepper
- Pinch chilli flakes

DIRECTIONS

1. Take the aubergine and cut the ends off, then cut it in half (lengthwise). Now cut each half into strips about 2.5 cm thick and 7 cm long. Take a medium bowl, add oil, aubergine, and seasonings, toss to coat.
2. Arrange a single layer into the Air Fryer basket. Cook 190°C 14 minutes, until golden, shake the basket once about halfway through.

Nutrition: Calories: 58; Fat: 3.5 g; Protein: 1 g; Carbs: 6.5 g; Fibre: 3 g; Sugar: 4 g

YORKSHIRE PUDDINGS

1 hour

18 minutes

4

INGREDIENTS

- 1 egg
- 4 tbsp (70 g) flour
- 4 tbsp (80 ml) milk
- 4 tbsp (80 ml) water
- 1/4 tsp salt

DIRECTIONS

1. Mix well all the ingredients together; you need to obtain a smooth batter with no lumps
2. Once the batter is ready, refrigerate for 30 to 60 minutes
3. Preheat the air fryer to 200 C
4. Grease a ramekin with some butter, then add a tsp of oil; heat at 200C in the air fryer for five minutes. This operation will prevent the batter from sticking
5. Once the ramekins are hot, add five tablespoons of Yorkshire Pudding mixture to each one
6. Cook at 200 C for 18 minutes
7. Do not open the air fryer while cooking!

Nutrition: Calories 89; Fat 2 g; Protein 4 g; Carbs 13 g; Fiber 2 g; Sugar 1 g

GREEN BEANS

2 minutes

7 minutes

2

INGREDIENTS

- 1 tsp. of lemon juice
- 1/2 tsp. of Garlic Powder
- 320 g of Fresh Green Beans
- 1 tsp. of Olive oil
- 1/2 tsp. of Salt
- 1/2 tsp. of Ground Pepper
- 1/2 tsp. of Italian Seasoning

Optional Garnish:

- Lemon Wedge
- Herbs- Parsley Thyme
- Chilli Flakes

DIRECTIONS

1. Trim the beans.
2. Prepare a seasoning mixture with all the ingredients except the beans.
3. Now pour the mixture on the beans, toss to coat well.
4. Preheat your Air Fryer at 200°C, 2 minutes.
5. Arrange the beans inside.
6. Air fry 7-8 minutes, 200°C.
7. Serve with optional garnish.

Nutrition: Calories: 50.5; Fat: 0.5 g; Protein: 2.5 g; Carbs: 10 g; Fibre: 4 g; Sugar: 4.5 g

CREAMY MASHED POTATOES

5 minutes

25 minutes

4

INGREDIENTS

- 900 baking potatoes (small to medium)
- 40 g butter
- 60 g cream cheese
- 2 stalks of fresh chives
- salt and pepper to taste

DIRECTIONS

1. Start by placing your potatoes into a foil packet, Layout your foil, then place the potatoes in them.
2. Air fry for 25 minutes at 200C. Check after 25 minutes if they are soft; The actual time will depend on the type of air fryer you have and the size of the potatoes.
3. Use a fork (or a potato masher if you prefer) to mash the potatoes.
4. Put the potatoes in a bowl.
5. Add the cream cheese and butter.
6. Add the chives and continue to mix. Continue mixing until the potatoes are mashed and the cream cheese and butter are combined.
7. Plate, serve and enjoy!

Nutrition: Calories: 322; Sugar: 3 g; Fat: 11 g; Carbohydrates: 50 g; Fiber: 5 g; Protein: 7 g

BRITISH VICTORIA SPONGE

15 minutes

28 minutes

8

INGREDIENTS

For the Victoria Sponge:
- 100 g Plain Flour
- 100 g Butter
- 100 g Caster Sugar
- 2 Medium Eggs

For the Cake Filling:
- 2 tbsp. Strawberry Jam
- 50 g Butter
- 100 g Icing Sugar
- 1 tbsp. Whipped Cream

DIRECTIONS

1. Preheat the Air Fryer to 180°C.
2. Grease a baking dish.
3. Cream the sugar and the butter until light and fluffy.
4. Now beat in the eggs, add a little flour with each.
5. Now gently fold in the flour.
6. Arrange your mixture into the tin and cook for 15 minutes, 180°C, then 10 minutes, 170°C.
7. Now leave it to cool and once it is cooled slice into two equal slices of sponge.
8. Now make the filling: Cream the butter, until you have a thick creamy mixture gradually add icing sugar and whipped cream.
9. Arrange a layer of strawberry jam, then a layer of cake filling, then add your other sponge on top.
10. Serve!

Nutrition: Calories: 243; Fat: 16.5 g; Protein: 3 g; Carbs: 21 g; Fibre: 1 g; Sugar: 12 g

CREAMY CHOCOLATE ECLAIRS

15 minutes

25 minutes

9

INGREDIENTS

Éclair Dough:
- 50 g Butter
- 100 g Plain Flour
- 3 Medium Eggs
- 150 ml Water

Cream Filling:
- 1 tsp. Vanilla Essence
- 1 tsp. Icing Sugar
- 150 ml Whipped Cream

Chocolate Topping:
- 50 g Milk chocolate (chopped into chunks)
- 1 tbsp. Whipped Cream
- 25 g Butter

DIRECTIONS

1. Preheat the Air Fryer to 180°C.
2. While it is heating up, place the butter in the water, melt over medium heat, using a large pan, then bring to the boil.
3. Now remove it from the heat and stir in the flour.
4. Place the pan again to the heat and stir into it forms a medium ball in the middle of the pan.
5. Transfer the dough to a cold plate so that it can cool. Once it is cool beat in the eggs until you have a smooth mixture.
6. Then make into éclair shapes and place in the Air Fryer. Cook for 10 minutes on 180°C and a further 8 minutes on 160°C.
7. While the dough is cooking make your cream filling: Mix with a whisk the whipped cream, vanilla essence and icing sugar until nice and thick.
8. Leave the eclairs to cool and while they are cooling make your chocolate topping – Place the milk chocolate, whipped cream and butter into a glass bowl. Place it over a pan of hot water and mix well until you have melted chocolate.
9. Cover the tops of the eclairs with melted chocolate and then serve!

Nutrition: Calories: 181; Fat: 13 g; Protein: 4 g; Carbs: 27.5 g; Fibre: 1.5 g; Sugar: 3 g

GINGER BISCUITS

 10 minutes

 16 minutes

 10-12

INGREDIENTS

- 270 g plain flour
- 2 tsp ground ginger
- 2 tsp baking soda
- 1 tbsp cinnamon
- ½ tsp salt
- 170 g butter room temperature
- 200 g white sugar
- 1 egg
- 85 g maple syrup
- 70 g sugar for coating the cookies

DIRECTIONS

1. In a large bowl, mix together the flour, ginger, baking soda, cinnamon, and salt.
2. In a second bowl, beat the butter with the sugar, egg, and maple syrup until creamy.
3. Combine the dry ingredients with the wet ones. Once everything is mixed, shape into small balls using your hands.
4. Flat each ball a little (the thicker the better!)
5. Preheat your air fryer at 150°C, and then air fry the cookies for 8 minutes at the same temperature.
6. Add 4-6 biscuits simultaneously (leaving space between each one). It is not necessary to rotate them.
7. Cook until hard on the outside but soft to touch when you press the biscuit.
8. Repeat steps 6-8 for the remaining cookies.
9. Let cool before eating and enjoy!

Nutrition: Calories 300; Fat 14 g; Protein 4 g; Carbs 45 g; Fiber 3 g; Sugar 25 g

LEMON BISCUITS

5 minutes

5 minutes

9

INGREDIENTS

- 100 g Butter
- 100 g Caster Sugar
- 225 g Self Raising Flour
- 1 Small Lemon (rind and juice)
- 1 Small Egg
- 1 tsp. Vanilla Essence

DIRECTIONS

1. Preheat the Air Fryer to 180°C.
2. Mix flour and sugar in a bowl. Add the butter and rub it in until your mix resembles breadcrumbs. Shake your bowl regularly so that the fat bits come to the top and so that you know what you have left to rub in.
3. Add the lemon rind and juice along with the egg.
4. Combine and knead until you have lovely soft dough.
5. Roll out and cut into medium sized biscuits.
6. Place the biscuits into the Air Fryer on a baking sheet and cook for five minutes at 180°C.
7. Place on a cooling tray and sprinkle with icing sugar

Nutrition: Calories: 205; Fat: 10 g; Protein: 3.5 g; Carbs: 26 g; Fibre: 2.5 g; Sugar: 10 g

SOFT CHOCOLATE BROWNIES

20 minutes

18 minutes

10

INGREDIENTS

- 125 g Caster Sugar
- 2 tbsp. Water
- 142 ml Milk
- 125 g Butter
- 50 g Chocolate
- 175 g Brown Sugar
- 2 Medium Eggs (beaten)
- 100 g Self Raising Flour
- 2 tsp. Vanilla Essence

DIRECTIONS

1. Preheat your Air Fryer to 180°C.
2. Prepare the chocolate brownies: Melt 100 g of butter and the chocolate in a bowl above a pan, over medium heat. Stir in the brown sugar, now add the eggs and then add the vanilla essence. Add the self-raising flour and mix well.
3. Pour the mixture into a greased dish that is of an appropriate size for your Air Fryer.
4. Cook into the Air Fryer for 15 minutes, 180°C.
5. While the brownies are cooking it is time to make the caramel sauce – Mix the caster sugar and the water in a pan on a medium heat until the sugar is melted. Then turn it up and cook for a further three minutes until it has turned a light brown colour. Take off the heat and then after 2 minutes add your butter and keep stirring until it is all melted. Then slowly add the milk.
6. Set the caramel sauce to one side for it to cool.
7. When the brownies are ready chop them into squares and place them on a plate with some sliced banana and cover with some caramel sauce.
8. Serve!

Nutrition: Calories: 249; Fat: 13 g; Protein: 3.5 g; Carbs: 30 g; Fibre: 1.5 g; Sugar: 21.5 g

FRUIT CRUMBLE

15 minutes

15 minutes

6

INGREDIENTS

- 75 g Plain Flour
- 33 g Butter
- 30 g Caster Sugar
- 1 Medium Red Apple
- 4 Medium Plums
- 50 g Frozen Berries
- 1 tsp. Cinnamon

DIRECTIONS

1. Preheat your Air Fryer to 180°C.
2. Take a suitable dish that will fit in your Air Fryer, then add the fruit. Peel and dice everything, check it is all of a similar size.
3. Place plain flour in a mixing bowl along with sugar and mix in the butter. Rub fat into the flour until your mixture resembles breadcrumbs.
4. Arrange your crumble mixture over the fruit and place into the Air Fryer.
5. Cook 15 minutes, 180°C.
6. Serve!

Nutrition: Calories: 141; Fat: 4.5 g; Protein: 1.6 g; Carbs: 24 g; Fibre: 2.5 g; Sugar: 13 g

MINI APPLE PIE

5 minutes

18 minutes

9

INGREDIENTS

- 75 g Plain Flour
- 33 g Butter
- 15 g Caster Sugar
- Water
- 2 Medium Red Apples
- Pinch Cinnamon
- Pinch Caster Sugar

DIRECTIONS

1. Preheat your Air Fryer to 180°C.
2. Start by making your pastry - place the plain flour and butter in a mixing bowl and rub the fat into the flour. Add the sugar and mix well. Add the water until the ingredients are moist enough to combine into a nice dough. Knead the dough well until it has a smooth texture.
3. Cover your pastry tins with butter to stop it sticking and then roll out the pastry and fill your pastry tins.
4. Peel, dice your apples, place in the tins. Sprinkle them with sugar and cinnamon.
5. Add an extra pastry layer to the top and make some fork markings so that they can breathe.
6. Cook in the Air Fryer for 18 minutes.

Nutrition: Calories: 85; Fat: 3 g; Protein: 1 g; Carbs: 13.5 g; Fibre: 1.5 g; Sugar: 6.5 g

SHORTBREAD CHOCOLATE BALLS

4 minutes

13 minutes

9

INGREDIENTS

- 175 g Butter
- 75 g Caster Sugar
- 250 g Plain Flour
- 1 tsp. Vanilla Essence
- 9 Chocolate chunks
- 2 tbsp. Cocoa

DIRECTIONS

1. Preheat your Air Fryer to 180°C.
2. Take a bowl and mix your sugar, flour, and cocoa.
3. Rub in the butter, knead well until you see a smooth dough.
4. Now divide into balls, place a chunk of chocolate into the centre of each one, make sure none of the chocolate chunk is showing.
5. Place your chocolate shortbread balls onto a baking sheet in your Air Fryer. Cook them at 180°C for 8 minutes and then a further 5 minutes on 160°C so that you can make sure they are cooked in the middle.
6. Serve!

Nutrition: Calories: 297; Fat: 18 g; Protein: 4 g; Carbs: 31 g; Fibre: 3.5 g; Sugar: 10 g

STRAWBERRY CUPCAKES

15 minutes

8 minutes

10

INGREDIENTS

- 100 g Butter
- 100 g Caster Sugar
- 2 Medium Eggs
- 100 g Self Raising Flour
- ½ tsp. Vanilla Essence
- 50 g Butter
- 100 g Icing Sugar
- ½ tsp. Pink Food Colouring
- 1 tbsp. Whipped Cream
- 40 g Fresh Strawberries (blended)

DIRECTIONS

1. Preheat the Air Fryer to 170°C.
2. Meanwhile, cream the sugar and butter using a large mixing bowl. Do this until your mixture is light and fluffy.
3. Add the vanilla essence and beat in the eggs one at a time. After adding each egg add a little of the flour. Gently fold in the remaining flour.
4. Add them to little bun cases so that they are 80% full.
5. Place them in the Air Fryer and then cook for 8 minutes on 170°C.
6. Meanwhile make the topping: Cream the butter and gradually add the icing sugar until you have a creamy mixture. Add the food colouring, whipped cream and blended strawberries and mix well.
7. Once the cupcakes are cooked, using a piping bag add your topping to them doing circular motions so that you have that lovely cupcake look.
8. Serve!

Nutrition: Calories: 231; Fat: 13 g; Protein: 2.5 g; Carbs: 26 g; Fibre: 1 g; Sugar: 19 g

APRICOT AND RAISIN CAKE

10 minutes

12 minutes

8

INGREDIENTS

- 75g dried apricots
- 4 tbsp orange juice
- 75g self-raising flour
- 40 g Sugar
- 1 egg
- 75g Raisins

DIRECTIONS

1. Preheat air fryer to 160°C
2. In a blender or food processor, puree the dried apricots and juices until smooth.
3. Put sugar and cake flour in another bowl and mix. Add a beaten egg to flour and sugar and mix together. Add apricot puree and raisins and keep mixing.
4. Spray a small amount of oil on a baking pan suitable for the air fryers. Transfer and flatten the mixture in it.
5. Cook in the air fryer for 12 minutes and check after 10 minutes. Use a metal skewer to check if it is done. If desired, return the cake to the air fryer and brown for a few more minutes.
6. Allow to cool, then remove from pan and slice.

Nutrition: Calories: 116; Fat: 1 g; Carbohydrates: 26 g; Fibre: 1 g; Sugar: 16 g; Protein: 2 g

INDEX

CREDITS

Thanks to https://www.flaticon.com/ for the icons

Printed in Great Britain
by Amazon

13727671R00047